Turtles and Their Care

*Keeping turtles
in the backyard.*

A FIRST BOOK

Franklin Watts, Inc.   575 Lexington Avenue   New York, N.Y. 10022

Turtles and Their Care

by John Hoke

Illustrated with photographs
Drawings by Barbara Wolff

To my son, Franklin
His efforts toward making this
book possible were invaluable

SBN 531-00696-4

Library of Congress Catalog Card Number: 78-98669
Copyright © 1970 by Franklin Watts, Inc.
Printed in the United States of America

3   4   5

Contents

Turtles and Their Care

Painted, red-bellied, and spotted turtles, and diamondback terrapin sunning in an indoor pond.

Introduction

When compared to all of the other animals on earth, turtles lead a relatively uneventful and quiet existence — and have done so for a long time. Turtles belong to the class of animals called reptiles, which also includes snakes, lizards, crocodiles, and the sphenodon — a primitive reptile found in New Zealand. Of this class, turtles are the oldest group — turtles crawled about on earth more than 250,000,000 years ago, and most species have changed very little since then.

Turtles today get along fairly well with the world around them. In the wild, their life is not too hard. Once they are fully grown they have few enemies that can do them much harm, and so most turtles live for many years. There are some turtles that live for as long as a century.

Of the nearly two hundred and fifty kinds of turtles on earth, few attract man's attention, except for those that may have a product value. So even where man is nearby, turtles fare reasonably well. There is one turtle, however — the green turtle — that has been so hunted for its food value that its numbers have been frighteningly reduced. But for the most part, man pays turtles little heed. Even so, man is no doubt the turtle's worst enemy, though usually not deliberately. Since turtles like to bask in the warmth of the morning sun and often do so on highways, countless numbers of them are run over by fast-moving vehicles. And all too frequently those kept as pets perish from lack of understanding care and attention.

The turtle's form and habits have a lot to do with why it has survived in time, when such large or aggressive reptiles as the dinosaur have died out. One thing in particular has played an important role in the turtle's survival — its remarkable shell. Many reptiles of the past

The turtle's remarkable shell has played a major role in its survival through time.

relied upon great size or aggressiveness for protection, but the unique armored shell of the turtle evolved to shield it from other animals that might prey upon it. The giant reptiles also had one common drawback: the bigger they became, the more special became their wants and needs. In time, all such enormous — and specialized — reptiles disappeared for one reason or another as their environment changed beyond their narrow ability to adapt to such change.

Most turtles do not rely on aggressive behavior to defend themselves. As they wander or swim about, they tend to keep out of harm's way rather than stand and do battle. And in case of an attack, freshwater turtles scoot into the water and out of sight, while land turtles simply pull back into their portable fortresslike shell.

Turtles, Tortoises, and Terrapins

There are three names used to describe turtles. In general, terrapins (an Indian word) are what most freshwater and brackish-water coastal turtles are called. Tortoise is the name almost always given to land turtles in the United States. The big marine turtles are always called "turtles." But today, to avoid confusion, calling them all turtles is quite proper.

Turtle Anatomy

Almost all turtles have a tough leathery or bone-hard shell that encloses the soft parts of their body. It is open at the front and rear ends to accommodate the head, tail, and legs. When danger threatens, many turtles pull these soft parts into the shell. In most cases the shell of a grown turtle is tough enough to make it difficult if not almost impossible for most animals to bite into. There is one interesting turtle called the box turtle that can pull in its legs and head and then com-

The box turtle (Terrapene) *can close up completely when it feels it is in danger, hence its name.*

The snapping turtle makes up with aggressiveness what it lacks in armor and must be handled with great care.

pletely close up its hinged shell. There are few animals that can pry open a box turtle's shell, and so it is one of the best protected of all turtles. With such protection, the box turtle need not be — and is not — aggressive.

The soft-shelled and snapping turtles, on the other hand, have not nearly enough armor to protect them, and they cannot pull very far back into their shell when attacked. But they make up for this weakness by being very aggressive toward their enemies. Both have strong jaws and can bite hard with alarming speed. There are not very many animals that will brave their tempers. In addition, the soft-shelled turtle is a fast swimmer. Of the two, the snapping turtle is the most formidable.

Most land turtles are very well covered and can pull themselves into their shells when they are attacked. Also, most of them have a hard scaly skin that covers any exposed legs and other soft parts. Because this protection is at the same time quite bulky, some turtles do not get around very fast. Land turtles in particular move quite slowly, and are inclined to stay in one area, so long as it provides for their wants. When they walk it is obvious that the shell is somewhat heavy and cumbersome, for they tend to lumber about, pushing their way through the weeds by sheer force, and occasionally tumbling down slopes or piles of rocks.

Should they land topsy-turvy, turning right side up can be quite a chore. Most manage it after a few tries by using their head and legs to flip themselves over. There are several kinds of land turtles, however, that may perish if turned on their backs, since their neck, arms, and legs are not long enough to give them the needed leverage, unless they are near something that will serve to help pry themselves over. If they become upside down when they are out in the sun, they may perish from the sun's heat, should they fail to right themselves soon.

Water turtles have less difficulty where shell bulkiness is concerned. Their shells are just as hard and bony as the shells of land turtles, but are lighter in weight and more flattened and streamlined so as not to slow the turtles down when they swim. Freshwater turtles, on land or in the water, can usually move much faster than land turtles.

Turtles use their heads and legs to flip themselves right side up.

The jagged lines are where the bones of the shell meet. The tweezers show one of the lamina, with the indented grooves in the shell behind it, where these horny layers come together.

The upper part of the shell is called the *carapace* (Spanish for "shield") and the bottom part is called the *plastron* (Italian for "breastplate"). The two are joined at both sides in many instances by a bony bridge. Sometimes the parts of the shell are rigidly joined into one solid piece. The shells of several kinds of turtles like the box turtle are not joined with a bridge, and they may be hinged to permit partial or complete closing of the shell when the turtle pulls in. The plastron of the box turtle is hinged so that it may close up from underneath. There is one African turtle whose carapace is hinged over the hind legs.

The carapace and plastron are made of bony plates (shields) that are closely fitted together. They are usually covered over with layers that are made of a horny material (laminae) much like that of fingernails. This outer layer is sometimes shed, or worn off, but as the turtle grows in size new material grows beneath the older laminae to cover the constantly enlarging bone of the shell.

The turtle's method of breathing was complicated by the development of this rigid protective covering. Many other animals draw in air by moving their ribs and expanding their chest, but turtles cannot use this technique. Other muscles have been developed instead to enable them to draw air into their lungs. Some aquatic turtles are also able to extract some oxygen directly through the skin from water. Land turtles can hold their breath for a considerable time and will obtain what oxygen they need from the air held in this way.

The turtles that have soft shells, or those that are leathery in composition, are aquatic and can move away from trouble more easily. They do not need the castlelike protection required by the slow-moving land turtles.

All Turtles Are Born from Eggs

Turtles mate shortly after their long winter hibernation (if they live in a temperate climate). In time, the female becomes gravid (swollen with eggs) and must find a place in the ground to lay her eggs. All turtles seek a proper place on land to dig a hole in which to lay their eggs. The choice is made with obvious care, for even water turtles will travel quite a distance from water to find a suitable place. The location picked is usually in the open because warmth from the sun is important for the development of the young turtle in the egg.

The turtle uses her hind feet to dig out a pot-shaped hole, as deep as her feet can reach. She then drops her eggs into the hole one by one, or several at a time. In some cases she arranges them with her hind feet as she lays them, and taps loose soil in about them. Once they are all laid (as few as several or as many as a hundred, depending on the kind of turtle) she pushes the soil dug from the hole back in place and

9

Eggs are laid in a hole the female digs, and are then covered over. Some turtles go to elaborate pains to make the finished nest look as natural as possible, so that the nest will not attract the attention of predators.

packs it down with her hind feet or plastron. When the job is done she departs. She plays no further role in the future life of the eggs or the turtles that will hatch from them.

The time it takes for bird eggs to hatch is quite exact, for they are kept warm by the warm-blooded bird. Turtles, being reptiles, are cold-blooded, and so cannot provide warmth for the eggs. The warmth turtle eggs receive comes from the surrounding earth, heated by sunlight and the weather, and so the time it will take them to hatch is quite varied. In general, as much as two or more months may pass before they hatch.

In a temperate climate, most eggs laid early in the spring or summer will hatch before cold weather sets in. Some turtles, however, may lay several clutches of eggs in the same year, and those laid later in the summer, or those laid earlier but that did not receive enough warmth because of unseasonable weather, may not incubate sufficiently to hatch during warm weather. Should they not hatch before cold weather sets in, they will remain dormant over the winter. Also, it is not unusual for some turtle eggs to hatch just before cold weather sets in. In this case the young turtles may stay in their buried nest, hibernate through the winter, and emerge the following spring.

The hatching itself is quite a chore. The shell of the egg is tough and often of a leathery quality, and it may be buried as much as a foot in the ground. When it is time to hatch, the hatchling must cut its way out of the egg. In order to do this, it grows what is known as an egg tooth on the end of its beak. With this special tool, the baby turtle pushes against the inner surface of the egg until it has worn an opening through which it can poke its head. Using its legs to help, it soon breaks out of the shell. Once free of the egg, the turtle laboriously digs its way up through the soil. The tooth is shed soon after.

It is at these times that turtles are the most vulnerable to attack

Snapping turtle emerging from egg. Normally, the turtle would still have to dig its way out of the dirt in the nest. Part of the yolk sac is retained after birth and continues to provide nourishment for the very young turtle.

from all kinds of predators. The mother turtle is often out of her protective element (particularly in the case of sea turtles) and the eggs themselves may be snatched up by predators even as they are laid. Even if safely buried they may yet be dug up by raccoons or skunks or humans. Or the weather may be dry for so long that the ground moisture will be too little to keep the eggs from drying out. Bad weather may also deprive the eggs of needed warmth for so long that the food energy of the developing embryo cannot be sustained. That any fair share of eggs are hatched at all is remarkable.

The ordeal of the tired newborn turtles is not over when they reach the surface. There they are prey for a host of prowling animals and birds. But newborn turtles are wary and secretive. Until they feel they are in their proper element, they do their best to avoid detection. Young water turtles seem to sense that the best direction to water is downhill. When sea turtles emerge from their sandy beach nest, they run down the beach to the water's edge. For them to be born in daylight is tragic, for they often run a gauntlet of diving frigate birds that swoop down and snatch them up. Of those turtles, if any, that do reach water, there are the predators of the deep to be wary of until the turtles grow too big to be swallowed in one gulp.

Once the turtles that survive all these hurdles are in their proper environment, life is a bit easier for them. With each passing day their chances for survival grow better.

If this unusual and harsh burden of birth suggests that their chances for survival are poor, remember one thing: once through all this, most turtles live a long time. Throughout their lives they will bear many clutches of eggs, from which the survival of only a handful of infant turtles is enough to perpetuate the species.

Land Turtles

Perhaps the largest and best-known land turtles are the Galápagos turtles. They live on a narrow archipelago in the Pacific Ocean off the coast of Ecuador. They grow to weigh hundreds of pounds and to a length of about three or more feet. And they can live for well over a century. This peaceful creature used to number in the thousands, but in the early days of sailing, seamen knew that these turtles could live for months without much care in the hold of a ship. As fresh meat was scarce on long voyages, passing ships would stop at the Galápagos Islands and take aboard many of these large turtles for food. Over the years they became scarce to the point where there was real danger that they would become extinct. Fortunately, conservationists encouraged the Ecuadorian government to halt indiscrimi-

Galápagos turtle
(Testudo)

nate trapping of this turtle and so some of the different kinds of Galápagos turtles have survived — though nowhere near their earlier numbers.

One of the most plentiful and widespread land turtles is the box turtle. It is found over much of the United States and is a peaceful inhabitant of woodlands, meadows and fields, and wet areas. Although of some trouble to farmers — it particularly likes strawberries and cultivated greens — it does little agricultural damage. In a way, it makes up for any damage done by eating insects and grubs that are harmful to farmers' crops.

Not a great deal is known about young box turtles, for as hatchlings they keep very much to themselves. Those who have found and cared for them claim that the infant box turtle is quite fond of meat — insects, worms, and slugs being readily eaten by them. As the box turtles grow larger (a little over half an inch a year) they begin to pay attention to vegetable matter and in time develop an interest in a wide assortment of leafy greens and fruits. Even banana peels and other exotic foods are eaten by them when kept as pets.

The box turtle is born not able to use its special plastral hinge. At birth, the plastron appears all in one piece, with little to show that the hinge will develop. As the turtle grows, its shell hardens, yet the plastron stays flexible at the proper juncture. Within several years the turtle can completely close up. When it does this, even a large dog can do little more than gnaw at the edges of the hard shell.

The box turtles' adaptive ability is almost limitless. Being reptiles, of course, they cannot stand subfreezing temperatures. In northern parts of the country they dig in and hibernate during the winter. A hole in the ground or a deep pile of leaves becomes their home for the winter, so long as the climate stays above freezing. Should the winter weather prove mild, they may come out on rare warm days to

14

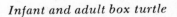
Infant and adult box turtle

look around, but they keep near their burrow so they can get back in before the cold of night returns.

They emerge in the warmth of spring, roaming about, eating worms, insects, and sprouting greens, and, in time, they mate. Late in the spring or in early summer the gravid females seek out an open place in which to dig a hole and bury the eggs where the sun will keep them warm. Once the female turtle has laid her eggs, she spends the rest of the warm season eating, sleeping, and wandering about.

Should it become unseasonably hot and dry, box turtles seek out a shady and moist place where it is cool and where they can obtain enough water to drink. It is not unusual to find as many as fifty box turtles within about one hundred feet of a stream or creek bed that divides large areas of open pasture or fields. They often burrow into the cool sand and mud of the stream bed to await the return of more temperate weather.

Box turtles are found mostly on land, yet they are quite fond of

Box turtles like water, although they have a very limited swimming ability.

water. They like to wade in shallow water or to float quietly, taking in the sun without getting too hot. This is a good time to observe their breathing. Since they can obtain enough oxygen from a single breath of air to sustain them for some time, they need not breathe in the rhythmic manner of most warm-blooded animals. While they float in the water they may hang their heads down, looking very much as though they were dead. But when it comes time to take a breath of fresh air, they raise their heads out of water to get it. They will take in one breath, let it out, and after repeating this action many times, will hold the last one for some time, extracting from it the oxygen needed over a period of time. When the turtle does this breathing exercise it bobs like a cork — rising and settling in the water as each quick breath is taken in and let out.

16

As much as box turtles like water, their swimming ability is no measure of their pleasure. In water too deep for them to wade in, they will flounce along with disorganized kicking, making very poor forward progress for all the effort. Compared to the swift, well-organized swimming of water turtles, box turtles present a comical sight as they paddle about.

As the season advances and the days and nights grow cooler, they tend to burrow down closer to the earth each night. And their nightly chosen place is bare from their digging in to get closer to the earth's warmth. During the day the sun's warmth is still great, so they forage about to fatten up on the fall harvest of berries and other low-hanging fruits they can reach or those that fall to the ground.

When winter comes in earnest, the ground becomes colder and colder, and so does the turtle. It seeks out a burrow in leafy mulch, beneath a fallen log or under an earthen bank. The colder it gets, the slower the turtle moves. All of its body processes slow down. Even its heartbeat drops to a very slow rhythm. Since it needs less oxygen, each breath lasts longer. In time it becomes dormant and almost lifeless in its winter burrow. And so in this state of suspended life — hibernation — it spends the cold of winter.

SOME LAND TURTLES

There are a great many more species of aquatic turtles than there are land turtles in the United States. Of the kinds of turtles that spend most of their time on land, the various box turtles, the gopher turtles, and the wood turtles are the major representatives of land turtles.

Gopher turtle
(Gopherus)

Gopher Turtles. There are three kinds found in the United States, all related to the Galápagos turtle (although they seldom exceed a foot in length). Able to live in arid places, the smaller member of this family — Berlandier's turtle — is found in southern Texas. The second member, the desert turtle, is found in Nevada. The third member, called the gopher turtle, is found in the southernmost states, from Florida and South Carolina west along the Gulf coast into Texas. The gopher turtle is able to dig deep burrows in the ground to escape unseasonable weather and to keep out of harm's way. It feeds on many forms of plant life, from fruits to cactus, and insects and small animals.

Wood turtle
(Clemmys insculpta)

Wood Turtle. A large but quiet and gentle turtle of the Great Lakes and New England, south to Virginia. It is not unusual for an adult to be 9 inches long. Its shell is markedly keeled and sculptured. Its legs are often a salmon-red color, and heavily plated with scales where exposed when it has pulled back into its shell for protection. Though it prowls the floor of forests and woods, it spends a fair amount of time in water and marshy areas, and in thickets and meadows looking for fruits, berries, vegetables, and mushrooms. Makes a fine pet and is easy to feed as it eats all kinds of meat and vegetables found in a supermarket.

Turtles That Live in the Water

The largest living turtle in the world is a sea turtle called the leatherback turtle. It can grow to over seven feet long and weigh almost a ton. Sea turtles spend their entire lives in the ocean. Most are larger than any land turtle. Only the Galápagos and Aldabra turtles and a few freshwater turtles such as the alligator snapping turtle rival the size and weight of the smaller sea turtles. Some kinds of sea turtles are few in number because they have been depleted by predators, while others that have economic value are preyed upon by man — their worst enemy.

Although they spend their lives at sea, they must come ashore to lay eggs. It is at this time that they are most vulnerable to attack, because they are so awkward and clumsy on land, and it is a wonder that they survive at all. Moreover, only a fraction of their hatchlings ever reach the water and mature.

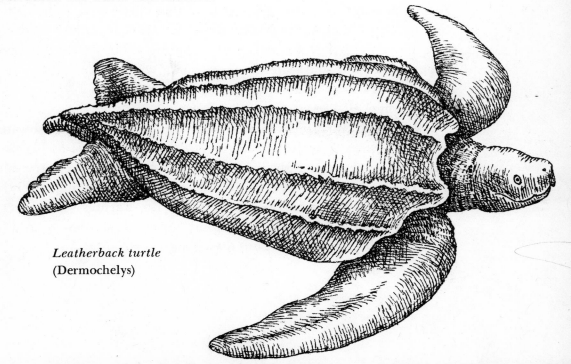

Leatherback turtle
(Dermochelys)

In the ocean, sea turtles are graceful creatures that seem to fly rather than swim in their watery environment. They are highly streamlined, and their front legs, moving in a winglike fashion, propel them through the water at speeds no other turtles can achieve. Some can navigate at better than fifteen knots and can maneuver well enough to make chasing them with a motorboat quite difficult.

Freshwater turtles, on the other hand, spend a major amount of their life in water, but they often leave the water to bask in the sun. Unlike sea turtles, their feet are equipped with claws so that they may climb out of water more easily. Many freshwater turtles, and such coastal turtles as the diamondback terrapins, have large hind feet that are webbed in much the same way as a duck's feet, so that their feet push them through the water efficiently.

The freshwater soft-shelled turtles that spend almost all of their time in water are particularly adapted to aquatic life. Their feet are fully webbed and their bodies are streamlined. Many spend much of their time buried in the silt or sandy bottom of streams, where they can snatch at fish or other bite-size food that chances by. When they want to dig in, they hover just above the sandy bottom and whip up the sand with their four feet while rippling their soft shell. They quickly settle into the water-loosened sand, which then settles upon them. When things quiet down, all that can be seen is a slight hump of sand and their eyes and snout sticking out just above it.

The alligator snapping turtle is one of the largest of freshwater turtles. It grows to well over a hundred pounds, and is as big as a truck tire. It is quite ugly in appearance. Although not a trouble-maker, when teased or bothered in its element it can bite severely.

The giant alligator snapper is found in the warmer southeastern parts of the United States. The snapping turtle is similar in appearance to the alligator snapper, but does not grow so large.

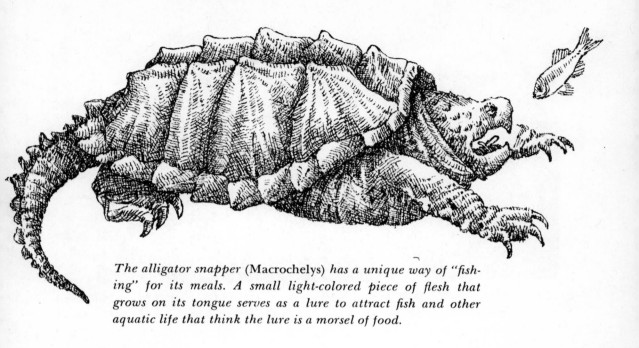

The alligator snapper (Macrochelys) *has a unique way of "fishing" for its meals. A small light-colored piece of flesh that grows on its tongue serves as a lure to attract fish and other aquatic life that think the lure is a morsel of food.*

Painted Turtles

There are four kinds of painted turtles — Eastern, Western, Southern, and Midland. Minor shell markings, color variation, and carapace shield positioning distinguish the four varieties, but in many respects they are quite similar in both their appearance and behavior. They are found almost everywhere in the country. They are so adaptable that they can hibernate over the winter if they live in a colder northern climate, or, in a warmer climate, they can stay active for much of the year. The temperature of the body of water in which the particular turtle lives largely determines how much time the

Painted turtles (Chrysemys), *basking on a log (under a lamp in an indoor enclosure).*

turtle may spend in hibernation. When the water drops much below 50°F., the body processes of the turtle slow down to where the turtle will need little or no food for long periods of time. And so it may spend the cold period in the muddy bottom of a stream, lake, or swamp — or in a muskrat tunnel or other burrow, under water.

In the spring, the earth becomes warmer, and so pond and lake water temperatures slowly begin to rise. Even though sunny spring days may still be brisk, the painted turtle climbs up on a log to bask in the warm sun. Being dark-shelled, it soon absorbs the sun's warmth, which frees it of the sluggish torpor of hibernation. Though the weather may still fluctuate, the temperature of the water in which it lives stays fairly constant, and slowly rises with the advance of spring. For a while, sunbathing remains the painted turtles' major early spring activity. Although they absorb considerable warmth with each sunning, they plunge back into water that is still cold and their body processes remain at a fairly low ebb. Their need for food is still not great — and should there be a cold snap, they may resume hibernation until it passes.

Small fish, frogs, and other life, still a bit sluggish from the cold, fall prey to those turtles that begin to forage for food. The hungry turtles may also eat leafy water plants and land plants close to the water.

Painted turtles mate in the water. Then, sometime between May or July, depending upon when spring begins in the part of the country the female lives in, she leaves the water to find a suitable place to lay her eggs. She may travel hundreds of feet away from the water to find the right place, and like other turtles she digs a hole for the eggs

There is considerable courtship during the mating of painted turtles. The male attracts the attention of the female by lightly brushing her cheeks with the back of his claws. He continues his attention until the female is prepared to mate.

with her hind feet. The usual number of eggs is less than ten, although some kinds of painted turtles may lay as many as a dozen or more. As she lays the eggs, she arranges each one in the hole with her hind feet. When the last egg is deposited, she rakes the dirt back into the hole and carefully packs it down with her feet and with pressure exerted with the plastron. After this process, which sometimes takes two hours, she returns to the water to join the other turtles in a lazy existence for the rest of the summer.

Painted turtles love to bask in the sun, and there are many among the usual crowd of turtles on logs in a pond on a sunny day. In the process of sunning, they become warm and dry, which is important,

Painted turtles, like this Western painted turtle, are avid sunbathers. They will stick their legs out as far as they can, so as to get as much exposure to the sun as possible. From time to time they twist their feet so that the sunlight falls on the underside. They even spread their toes apart so that the webbing between them is also exposed to the sun.

for it discourages the growth of fungus and other moisture-supported freshwater organisms in the water.

They present an idyllic picture of contentment, apparently free of care. But they are wary all the while and are alert to preying birds, or a boat that may come too close. When this happens, they splash into the water and the safety of the muddy bottom below, to emerge when the danger is over.

During the summer the turtles feed on insects floating on the water and whatever they can catch that swims in the water or burrows in the mud of the pond. They also eat the leaves and stalks of the many kinds of leafy water plants that grow in ponds and lakes.

When winter approaches, the temperature of their watery habitat steadily falls. Sunbathing forestalls its effects for a while, but the long nights in the steadily cooling water lower the body process rate. The turtles become increasingly torpid and spend more and more time in the depths of the cooling water. In time, only the heat of a brilliant sun on a clear day — penetrating to the bottom, should the water be clear — stirs them to come to the surface for another bask in the sun. But when the gray days of winter descend in earnest, the painted turtle joins the other cold-blooded pond creatures in hibernation.

The box turtle and the painted turtle are probably the most widely distributed land and water turtles in the United States. This is why they were selected to show the life of a typical land turtle and a typical aquatic turtle. In general, most other turtles on the continent share a similar land or aquatic existence. There are, of course, different living conditions for each kind of turtle. And some other land turtles are almost as aquatic as the painted turtle. But even with these differences among the species, their way of life falls into one or the other of these two general patterns of living.

SOME AQUATIC TURTLES

There are many kinds of aquatic turtles in the United States. Among some of the better known and most widely distributed are:

Mud turtle
(Kinosternon)

Mud Turtle. Most are found throughout the lower half of the United States. Although not a colorful turtle (its shell is usually brownish and without a marked pattern) it is an amusing creature. In the wild it feeds on water insects, larvae, and other small animals it can catch. Easily kept in an aquarium, it will eat a wide variety of foods, such as hamburger and other bits of meat. Its plastron is hinged like a box turtle's. It is a gentle animal that seldom bites, and the infant mud turtle gets along well with other turtles.

Musk Turtle. In the same family as the mud turtle, it derives its name from a slight odor it may release when disturbed or frightened. Its shell is more domed than that of the mud turtle and its head markings are more distinctive. It has much the same habits as the mud turtle, but spends a lot of time foraging on the bottom of the water for food. It also makes a fine aquarium pet. It seldom grows longer than 4 inches; infants barely cover a nickel when just out of the egg.

Musk turtle
(Sternotherus)

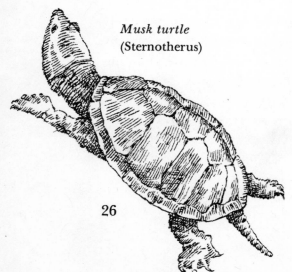

26

Snapping Turtle. Ugly in appearance, its shell is rough and sometimes ridged. The head seems too big for its body, and is beaked in a way that accurately suggests that it has an aggressive personality. The adult is quite large and heavy. At over 30 pounds and 18 inches it is a dangerous animal to trifle with. When on land or provoked when captured, it can inflict serious bites. It does not behave this way in the water: here, unless severely provoked, it avoids trouble, and does not offer much risk to unwary swimmers wading in the water. It is fond of fish, frogs, and whatever else it can catch. Infants make fine tank pets and develop none of the aggressive attitude of their elders in the wild. They get along well with larger turtles, but with other turtles present, they are sometimes too slow in their eating to get a fair share of the food.

Soft-shelled Turtle. Of all freshwater turtles, it is the best adapted to aquatic life, being highly streamlined with the most paddlelike feet. Shell softness stems from a leathery, soft skin that covers the bone of the shell underneath, instead of the horny layer of laminae that covers other turtles' shells. It grows quite large, to well over 30 pounds, with a shell diameter of over 18 inches. Being bad tempered and quite slippery, it is difficult to handle a large one without risk of being bitten. It will eat most anything it can catch. Infants adapt reasonably well to an aquarium, but do not do well with other turtles their own size. They will eat dried fish food but relish an occasional earthworm and pieces of fish.

Snapping turtle
(Chelydra)

Soft-shelled turtle
(Amyda)

Slider
(Pseudemys)

Slider. This is one of the most popular turtles for pets and is the one most available in pet stores. Most popular is the elegant slider. Infants are a bright green, profusely laced with yellow and lighter green lines on both head and body. Their most distinguishing feature is a brilliant red earmuff-shaped flash of red along each side of the head — hence their popular name, Red Ear. They are found in midwestern and southern states, near slow-moving rivers and ponds. Living habits are similar to those of painted turtles.

Red-bellied Turtle. One of the larger members of the slider family, it grows up to 16 inches long. The red coloration on the plastron is marked in the infants, but fades to yellow with age. It makes an excellent pet, becomes quite tame, and will eat a variety of foods — vegetable greens particularly.

Red-bellied turtle
(Pseudemys rubriventris rubriventris)

Map turtle
(Graptemys geographica)

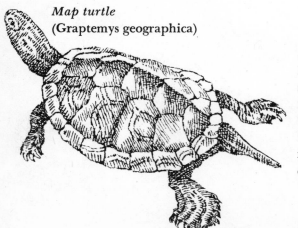

Map Turtle. Found in the eastern half of the United States from around the Great Lakes states south into the states between Texas and Alabama, it is bigger than the painted turtle, but more timid and difficult to approach. Its name stems from yellow-lined maplike patterns in the shell. It eats freshwater mollusks and crayfish, along with other animals and fish.

Diamondback Terrapin. It prefers salt and brackish tidewater areas and so is found only in coastal areas — from New England to the Texas gulf coast. The angular configurations of its shell give it its name. Not large, adults may grow to 9½ inches long. Because of its delicious flesh, it was once hunted until it was considered an endangered species. Young are now protected in several states; many of those marketed now come from special turtle farms, and it is less in jeopardy than it was. Particularly gentle, it makes a fine pet among other turtles of the same size. Interesting coloration of its head and skin — seldom any two with the same "facial" expression. Though prone to contract fungus disorders found in unclean freshwater, it will fare well in a clean, filtered freshwater tank and will eat much of what other turtles eat. Also likes an occasional piece of raw fish.

Spotted Turtle. This small turtle, seldom over 5 inches long, lives in the small streams and ponds of the Great Lakes, New England, and eastern coast states. Its black carapace is often speckled with orange-yellow spots. It eats aquatic insects and larvae and small animals. It will also eat an occasional tadpole or earthworm (which it must take into the water to eat). Although aquatic, it spends most of its waking hours basking in the sun — or under a lamp in an aquarium. Makes a good pet, but males often become aggressive toward other males so care must be taken to avoid injuries.

Diamondback terrapin
(Malaclemys)

Spotted turtle
(Clemmys guttata)

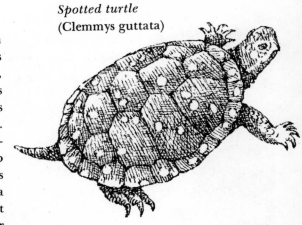

29

Keeping Turtles at Home or in School

Interest in turtles has risen so that most pet stores and tropical fish and aquarium supply stores now sell them. Turtles from other countries are being imported for sale through these outlets because interested buyers want to learn about the many interesting and colorful varieties found in other parts of the world. Unfortunately, the keeping of turtles as pets has yet to become the fine art that tropical fish-keeping has become in the past fifty years. All too frequently a newly acquired pet turtle is placed in little more than a shallow bowl of water or in a bare box. Just as frequently, kept in such poor quarters, the turtle languishes away to an untimely end.

The key to the successful keeping of turtles as pets is the same as that for keeping tropical fish: their quarters must be a healthy environment instead of an imprisoning container; a reasonable measure

The key to the successful keeping of turtles as pets is a healthy environment that offers important aspects of their own home in the wild.

of the conditions native to their own home environment must be provided; the turtles' biological needs and wants must be faithfully attended to. Aquarists have long been able to provide for these basic requirements for two reasons. They have come to know a great deal about the living requirements and behavior of tropical fish, and excellent low-cost equipment is now marketed to create a suitable artificial environment for tropical fish. Because of this success, some forms of tropical fish that a generation ago could not be easily kept alive out of their own environment have since been bred in aquariums.

Compared to what has been written about tropical fish-keeping, little has been published about keeping turtles healthy out of their home habitat. And except for certain fish-keeping equipment that will also provide for some of the wants of aquatic turtles, there is very little equipment being marketed specifically to meet the specialized requirements of turtles.

Fortunately, an increasing amount is now being published about turtles' behavior and their environmental needs. It is also relatively easy to build the special environments called for since most of the basic materials required are in common supply. And industry has long been marketing equipment such as small pumps, lights, or heaters that can be used to build the proper environment for keeping turtles happy and healthy. Although the manufacturers designed this equipment to serve other uses, a wise choice of certain items makes it possible to install a low-cost system with effective control of temperature and humidity, adequate lighting, and effective water-filtering techniques — all of which play an important role in the keeping of turtles out of their home environment. Tropical fish-keeping began in just this way years ago — making do with what was available — and the same technique applies today. The only difference is that the choice of materials and equipment is better today.

Turtles in the Yard

A large yard is not required for the space needed to make a satisfactory outdoor enclosure for turtles. Most turtles, native to the area, will exist quite happily in a small fenced-off area that confines them, yet is adequate for their needs. The location selected should have both shaded areas and places that are open to the sun throughout the day. While a flat place in the ground will serve, it is best if there is some difference in the land level inside the enclosure, with the higher areas exposed to the sun. It is desirable to choose a part of the yard through which water normally flows, where a banked area can be included to serve as the higher dry place. Most turtles also like a moist place, preferably complete with a little mud wallow in which they may burrow to escape the summer heat. If lack of all-day shade is a problem, shrubs should be planted near the low area.

Most turtles will exist happily in a small fenced-off area that confines them, yet cares for their needs.

A low fence is needed to keep the turtles from wandering off. For box turtles and others about the same size, wire fencing of the kind used to edge flower gardens works well. It is high enough to keep them from crawling over it without making the area look like a pen. The mesh shown is narrow enough to keep larger turtles from crawling through, yet it is not so fine as to give them footing to climb over the fence. The roll of fencing illustrated is as it comes from the store. It is twice as wide as is needed, but can be cut down the middle to make two lengths of the right height — twice as long as the original roll, but able to confine all but the largest turtles.

There are some turtles, notably gopher turtles, that may burrow under such an obstruction if they feel too confined. But if they are given lots of room with adequate shade, they will be happier with their quarters and will do remarkably little burrowing. The openness of this kind of large-mesh fencing deceives most turtles and they will try to go through it rather than dig under it.

Where there is the risk of burrowing, however, there are two ways to prevent the turtles from getting out. One is to use a taller fencing, such as the whole width of the original uncut roll, and to bury several inches of one edge in a narrow trench dug around the area to be enclosed. The other way is to make wire U-clips and to sink them in at each point in the mesh of the fence. This in effect extends the fence into the ground without any digging. Taking care to space the clips well will keep a burrowing turtle from getting through. The latter method is neater and does not damage a lawn.

Many turtles, particularly box turtles, require water, not only to drink but in which to wallow. If the low-fenced part of the yard has no wet area, a square of sod can be cut out and replaced by a shallow plastic or aluminum pan large enough to take care of the number of turtles it is desired to keep. The pan should be sunk in the earth so

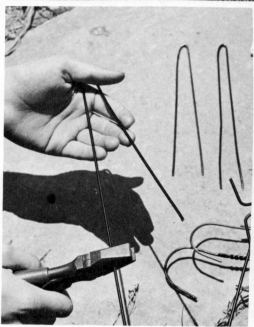

Cut down the middle strands alternately so that each resulting half-width roll has a series of pointed wire "stakes" that will pin the fencing in the ground. These wire stakes, however, are not adequate to hold the fence on the ground: add U-shaped wire stakes at approximately each foot of fence to anchor it. Make the U-clips from galvanized wire or coat hangers, each about 6" long. Hammer them in so that they grip the bottommost wire edge of the fence. Wire together the fencing ends where they meet on the circle.

Since the fence appears so "open" turtles will try to get through it rather than dig under it.

that its rim is level with the ground to make it easy for the turtles to get in and out — and so that the pan can be easily flushed out with a garden hose.

If the low place in the pen is an area where water normally settles, only a small bit of sod need be cut out to create a shallow mud wallow. If permissible, a few bricks or rocks can then be cemented in to create a natural-looking wallow that will hold water.

Feeding in the pen should be done in an open place where leftover food can be seen and removed, or washed away with a hose.

The finished pen will provide an ideal outdoor environment for such local turtles as box turtles. A shaded area will give them relief from the sun during the strong heat of the day, and where possible, some of this shade should cover part of the pan or mud wallow.

35

The high and open place in the fenced area provides a place for sunning on cooler days, and a place in which female turtles will be likely to lay their eggs. Being higher than the rest of the pen, there is less chance of the eggs being washed out or drowned by too much groundwater in wet weather.

The hatching of eggs does pose a problem where this system of fencing is concerned. Large-mesh fencing will not confine hatchling turtles. To keep them in the pen, the entire fence will have to be lined with a new fence of 5-inch high, ½-inch wire hardware cloth staked in close to the ground with coat-hanger U-clips, one inch outside the fence. Since this kind of wire can be climbed by nimble infant turtles, the top inch of this fence will have to be bent inward toward the big mesh fence, so that the hatchlings cannot make their way out over the top. Of course, a smaller pen for hatchlings can be made elsewhere, or within the larger pen, using the ½-inch hardware cloth.

Water Turtles in the Yard

A small pond in a yard is an ideal place in which to keep and study water turtles. However, these turtles will need to be confined, if they are to be kept from wandering off. It is true that the presence of the pond will encourage them to stay — for want of a better place — but should they be newly caught, and thus be more bothered by nearby people, passing vehicles, or any other disturbance, they will leave if not fenced in. The same kind of fencing already described will work with water turtles that are not too large to climb over it. With an existing pond, it is best to allow considerable space between the pond's edge and the fence, so that the scene does not appear crowded.

When a turtle is through laying eggs, cap the nest with a "hat" fashioned from wire hardware cloth, and stake it down with U-clips. This prevents predators from digging the eggs up. Two infant box turtles are shown in this nest, with the "hat" lifted away.

Water turtles like to wander about, and also need a place on land to lay eggs.

If both land and water turtles are to be kept, and there is no pool in the yard, the planning for an appropriate yard location differs little from that for keeping land turtles. It is only necessary to provide enough added area for the pond.

Ideally, a natural water runoff area is the place to locate the pond — provided it is not a running river that would wash away everything in a storm. If there is risk of this, another "low" in the yard that suffers less from storm runoff should be chosen.

Digging out the pond and carting away soil are chores of family-size proportions. But with the help of family and friends, the pond can be dug and concreted in a day. However, it may be necessary to

37

hire a firm, or professional gardener, to put it in, as the cementing requires some experience.

From an aesthetic point of view, an oval- or kidney-shaped pool is best. It should be at least six feet long — the oval dimension being about four to five feet across. It need not be more than eight to ten inches deep, but the middle should be more than two feet deep if winters are cold and the turtles are left out to hibernate. In any event, the bottom near the rim should be shallow so that if a small child should chance to step in, getting out will not be a problem.

The sides of the pond should be sufficiently sloped so as to make it easy for the turtles to climb out of the pond. The cement rim should have a uniform height all the way around. One end of the oval, or kidney, should be a long, beachlike slope, so that box turtles can easily enter and leave the water.

Raw concrete is rough and therefore hard on the plastrons of larger turtles. Several kinds of latex-based swimming-pool paints are sold to cover rough concrete and will correct this problem.

Water plants can be put in the pond, along with hyacinth and other floating plants. Sufficient plants should be provided since greens comprise much of a water turtle's diet. If there are many large turtles in the pond, the hyacinth may prove to be the only plant life that will reproduce fast enough to keep ahead of their appetites.

Since turtles are fond of sunbathing — and often feel more secure sunning in the middle of a pond than on its edge — a small log should be anchored in the middle of the pond for them to crawl out upon.

Alternatives to a concrete pond are plastic liners (sometimes complete with pump and waterfall) that are sold in garden-supply stores. They must be buried in the ground. Aside from the digging involved, this is decidedly an easier solution. However, there are two drawbacks to their use. One is that they may not be big enough to handle the number and size of turtles it is planned to house. Secondly, the plastic pond is not easy for turtles to crawl out of, and a wooden ramp of some sort must be added so that turtles may have easy access to and from the water. For those who feel it would be adequate, however, these liners are worthy of consideration for building a modest pond.

The outdoor turtle pen has much to offer for the effort expended. Aside from the compelled confinement of the fence, the environment is natural. The collector need only attend to the diet and health needs of the turtles, keep things clean, and protect them.

There are sometimes problems where protection is concerned: mostly ones of marauding dogs, cats, raccoons, and unknowing neighborhood children who do not realize that the turtles they "find" in a neighbor's yard belong there. Keeping the area clean has much to do with discouraging nighttime animal prowlers. The smell of un-eaten food in the pen will attract them from long distances. Watering the grass in the pen frequently will wash away any food odors that might attract the dogs, cats, and raccoons.

The question of neighborhood children taking home what seems to them to be a stray turtle is another thing. The best approach is to generate their interest in what is being done, and to let them enjoy the turtles, too. They should be encouraged to catch a turtle of their own, and perhaps be permitted to keep it with the neighbor's collection, if need be, until they perhaps decide they would like a pen in their own yard.

Another concern involves routine yard maintenance — particularly if much of the yard is fenced and contains numerous turtles. Care must be taken when mowing the grass in the pen. All turtles should be accounted for before running a power mower through the grass.

A final concern is how to carry the outside collection of turtles through the winter season in colder areas. Since they are confined to

39

Trading turtles is part of the fun.

the yard, their ability to fend for themselves is limited. A place must be provided where they can hibernate without risk of their freezing to death.

The land turtles can be provided with a burrow in a steep bank, if it is deep enough to reach below frost line. If this is not practical, a deep pile of leaves, six feet or more in diameter, offers the same haven. It must be at least eighteen inches deep; more if the winter weather goes below zero. Badminton netting can be used to secure the pile of leaves, but it is not advisable to use tarpolin or plastic sheeting, because moisture from snow and rain falling on the pile is essential to turtles' survival. When frosty weather arrives, it is important to make sure that the land turtles go deep into the pile. On subsequent warm days, when they come back out to sun, a check should be made to see that they return to the pile at night.

The native water turtles will go into the pond. To make sure ice does not crack the pond, a few floating logs or plastic bottles should be put in the water for the winter. When the pond ices over later, leaves should be added to the pond. In the spring, this will all have to be cleaned out, but the added insulation will ensure the turtles' survival. It is essential to check frequently during the winter to be sure the pond stays full of water. The water turtles will hibernate at the bottom of the pond for the winter, and emerge with the return of spring. They should not be disturbed during this time, unless they are to be brought into an indoor pond for the rest of the winter season.

An outdoor pen can be as small or as large as a person wishes it to be, within the confines of his yard — or joined with that of a neighbor who shares his interest in keeping turtles. The yard can remain normal in appearance, but the turtles will stay in it where they can be watched as a part of your home environment, brought in from the wilderness.

Pile up leaves in the pen in which turtles will spend the winter, shielded from freezing weather.

Turtles Indoors

When turtles are brought indoors, providing a healthy environment for them becomes more involved. Indoors, *all* of their environmental needs have to be provided for, and many of them are quite necessary if the turtles are to be kept healthy.

Both land and water turtles have several essential and basic requirements that must be provided in an indoor facility if they are to survive in health. They must have access to both dry *and* humid warmth. They must have a choice of foods that will meet their full dietary needs. Their living quarters must not be cramped and crowded and must be kept clean. The quarters should also include places of relatively dark seclusion wherein they can feel safely hidden. This private place should not be disturbed unless the need to handle the turtles is great. Their continued good health and natural behavior cannot be assured if these basic conditions are not provided.

In establishing indoor facilities for keeping turtles as pets and for study, every effort should be made to set up their new environment so that they can settle into it quickly, and so that they need not be needlessly handled and shifted about in the routine of caring for them. Most turtles do not fare well when they are frequently disturbed, and must be allowed to live with a minimum of handling. This is not to suggest that they are so fragile that the keeping of them will not be an enjoyable experience — that they can never be handled or that close contact cannot be made with them. What is important — particularly at the beginning — is that they should come to feel that their new home is one where they can feel safe and secure. Once they have accustomed themselves to life in a basically good indoor living environment, and are obviously content with it, then occasional handling for observation or friendly contact will not disturb them. When they are returned to their quarters they should be able to scoot off to some supposed hiding place — content that they are safe in it. They will develop an independence of behavior that is a real part of their life in the wild. As long as they are able — as pets — to exhibit this same behavior, an occasional handling will do them little harm. And, in time, it will lead to a form of healthy confident tameness that will replace the timidness many captive turtles will exhibit when first put in their new indoor quarters.

Providing an ideal indoor environment does not necessitate making a swamp or woodland glade out of a recreation room. But it does mean that a simple boxed-in enclosure will not do at all, for this would be little more than a prison in which turtles would be unhappy, and likely to perish. When the study of their natural behavior is an important consideration, if they are not completely happy in their new environment they will not exhibit the natural behavior in which the collector may be specifically interested.

Creating the proper environment in your home or schoolroom is not difficult, but it does require the use of some special, necessary equipment, as well as periodic care and attention — with no long periods of neglect. If turtles are to be kept indoors — particularly in wintertime — a specific amount of time must be devoted to taking care of their daily needs. The rewards for doing so are great.

Water Turtles, in an Indoor Pond

It takes surprisingly little effort to create attractive indoor environments for water turtles — from little tabletop puddles, for a few infant turtles, up to large, six-foot-in-diameter ponds that house twenty or more large turtles. The bigger pond is recommended for the more serious collectors willing and able to devote the time, effort, and space to building it, and for schools where active study of such wildlife warrants setting up a large system. The cost of electric power is great enough to be carefully weighed against the returns to be gained for the effort, however. It can involve as much as ten dollars a month for the food and the electric power needed to run the water, heating, lights, and filtering equipment in a large tank (particularly during the winter season, in colder climates).

The choice of environment size is great, however, and among the

A small tank with its own filter and high-intensity lamp. Small potted swamp plants survive well in a small system, where turtles cannot eat the leaves.

Attractive indoor environments can be small tabletop puddles or six-foot-in-diameter ponds.

ranges of those shown here, there is one that will serve most any interest and budget.

No matter how few or small the turtles, their container of water must be ample in size, and must be kept clean and warm. A simple bowl can be used to house a few small turtles, but it is difficult to keep such a bowl clean and warm without a great deal of extra effort. The water must be changed almost daily, to ensure cleanliness, and this of course requires taking the turtles out of the container for each cleaning. It is obvious that a turtle, so handled, can never settle down to a routine living pattern. And unless the room itself is quite warm, the water in such a container will seldom be warm enough — particularly in air-conditioned houses, or in wintertime.

The best water medium for keeping turtles is one that is both filtered and heated. These requirements can be provided with simple equipment that can be bought or made.

Choice of suitable containers is no problem, for many kinds and sizes are available for commercial and home uses. While tropical-fish aquariums can be used to house certain water turtles, they do not generally provide the best space configurations. The most suitable are those that offer lots of area with relatively little depth, like the larger plastic containers used to bathe babies or to mix cement, and the many different plastic wading pools. All are shallow compared to their area. They are pondlike and thus the best suited for containing the water medium in which turtles will live.

Keeping the water warm is no problem, for any of a number of commercial aquarium heaters will take care of this need. All are sold to meet given water volume requirements. Once the container size has been selected, the water content should be determined, and then a thermostatically controlled aquarium heater should be purchased, suited to keep that much water at the right temperature (above

75°F.). It may be necessary to construct some form of fixture to hold it in position in the tank, since most commercial aquarium heaters have a clamp intended for attaching them to the narrow rim of an aquarium, and are too small for a large-rimmed plastic tank.

Most small containers can be placed upon a bureau, bookcase, or substantial table, as with aquariums. A rubber or plastic mat should be placed under the tank as insurance against water damage. Larger wading-pool-type containers will have to occupy floor space in the home or schoolroom, and the power involved to keep it warm becomes an important cost factor: If located on a concrete floor, the bottom should be insulated with a sheet of fiberboard or plywood. Or a low, well-braced waterproofed platform of pine struts and plywood should be built, to raise it an inch or so from the concrete. This will help to keep heat loss and the cost of the power down. Treat the platform with a good waterproof finish to prevent mildew or wood rot from developing between the tank and the platform.

Keeping the water clean is of vital importance. No matter how big or small the container, a filter is needed to keep the water in it clean.

Turtles should be fed *in* their water. Much that has been written earlier discourages this, for without filtration the water becomes fouled by any uneaten food that is left in the tank. On the other hand, feeding turtles in a separate container requires handling them, which amounts to continually disturbing them in their environment. By providing a way to filter the water in which they live, they can be fed in their environment and yet things can be kept clean.

Some of the filtering equipment sold in tropical-fish stores will do a reasonable job of this, but few will take care of one important task: the effective removal of surface oils that collect on the water over a space of time. Turtles require some fish in their diet, and oil is re-

47

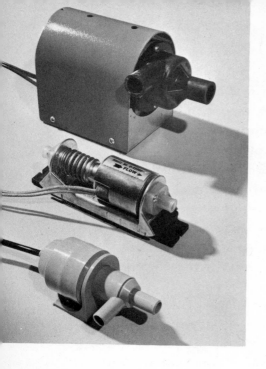

Three of the four pumps listed in the Materials List on page 84. All have been selected because they have both the necessary input and output fittings and their various pumping ratios are suitable for the different-sized systems mentioned. Of course, many kinds of pumps can be adapted for this purpose.

leased by the fish — and by the waste matter the turtles deposit in the water. A special oil-collecting filter is required for this, and has to be built.

A water pump is needed to circulate the water through the filter. There are many kinds of small water pumps on the market that are used for small garden fountains, and in connection with other commercial applications — including several kinds of better aquarium filters that feature turbine-operated water pumps. Most of these are open-input, sump-type pumps, however, that cannot be easily adapted to suck water through a piece of tubing, and then to push it out through a similar tube. This is an important requirement to meet in choosing the pump used to operate the turtle-tank filter.

In all of the systems shown, the method of pumping and filtering the water is the same. The water in the tank is drawn through the filter by the pump and returned back to the tank, free of oil and suspended sediment. In the process, considerable aerobic bacterial processing of the water also takes place. In many respects, the filter is really a miniature sewage-processing plant. In brief, it supports beneficial bacteria that are present in water. The bacteria biologically break down the many forms of waste products that collect in a system in which animal and plant life live. This includes processing uneaten food that would spoil. The water moving continuously through the filter ensures good aeration of the water and supports a healthy culture of this bacteria.

Much of the culture forms naturally on the filter rock soon after the filter is in use. The bacteria convert organic waste matter into harmless gasses, silty suspended matter, and soluble by-products of its water-purifying task. It would be impractical and too costly to create a small system able to remove all the by-products of this breakdown process, so the water has to be changed occasionally. But even with the collection of certain by-products in the water, it will last quite a while. When the water discolors to a slight yellow-amber, it is time to change it. Total replacement can be made, or a partial change each week or so, to stretch the process out to where it may never be necessary to make a one-time, total change of the water.

The pump can be hooked into the system in two ways.

(1.) The pump may be mounted on a bracket located near the tank rim, with a tube or hose connecting the filter to the input of the pump, and another hose directing the output water to create a streamlike action for the turtles that like the "exercise" of swimming into such a stream. The end of the output hose can be held on the bottom of the tank between several rocks. This directs the output in the direction desired and keeps the turtles from pushing the hose

The filter is constructed so that surface oil flows into it and is collected in the plastic sponge material that serves as a trap for oil and sediment in the water. Since oil floats across the surface of the water, the water must fall about half an inch as it flows into the filter, so that it "cascades," much like a dam spillway. The two narrow slits cut into opposite sides of the plastic filter bottle are thin so that the pump tries to pull more water out of the filter than flows into it. This causes the water level in the filter to drop below that of the water in the tank. The water will flow through the slits and fall "downhill" and the oil that was on the water cannot float back out.

(A) Rock to weight the filter. This one also serves as a ramp on which turtles may bask.

(1) Plastic bottle or similar cylindrical container. Cut (a) two slits below the rim of the bottle through which tank water will flow into the container and a hose hole at the bottom of the container where the pump will draw the water out of the filter.

(2) Piece of 1"-thick polyethylene sponge material for filter.

(3) Platform made from a circular piece of ⅛" plexiglass on which the filter sponge is placed. Drill ¼" holes in the platform, including a center hole. Cement a thin plastic rod (b) in the center hole to use as a lifting rod for pulling the sponge out of the filter bottle when it is to be cleaned or replaced with a clean filter. (A hole in the center of the sponge allows it to be slid into place over the rod and onto the platform.)

50

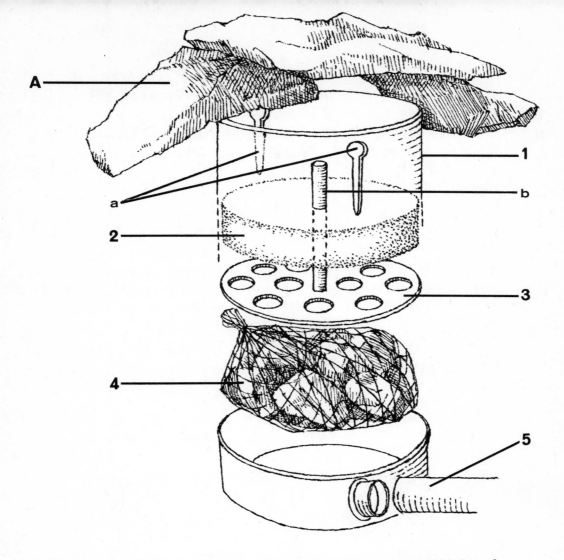

A

1

b

a

2

3

4

5

(4) Small pile of rocks or coarse construction gravel (not smooth pebbles); each about 1″ long. This gravel supports some of the aerobic bacteria culture that forms naturally shortly after the filter is used.

(5) Plastic tube or piece of garden hose (for larger systems) is pushed into the hole in the bottom of the filter bottle and connects to the input of the pump.

about. This setup is the one usually used with larger systems and the larger pumps shown in the Materials List.

(2.) Pump No. 3 in the Materials List can be bulkhead-mounted through a hole in the side of the main tank, near its bottom. With this method of mounting the pump, a hose from the filter to the pump input is all that is required to create a water circuit. An even, snug hole should be cut in the tank wall, so that the pump will fit tightly into place. To ensure a tight and leakproof mounting, silastic rubber should be smeared on the rim of the pump housing (the part that will make contact with the outside surface of the tank). The nozzle of the pump — with its input and output tubes — will hold the pump body in place through the tank wall. The mounting bracket that comes with the pump should be discarded. Should the plastic tank be some-what thin-walled, the foot of this mounting bracket should be cut off and the remaining piece used as an inside mounting washer to strength-

Pump and heaters shown mounted over the rim of a large floor tank. Filter sponges go into the container and are changed when they become too clogged to allow a free flow of water through them.

Bulkhead pump mounting

en the "sandwich" created between this washer, the tank itself, and the pump housing outside. The washer should be put in place on the threaded pump hole in the same way it came off the pump before it was cut for this use.

Setting Up the Indoor Environment

When all the proper equipment is ready, the assembling of the finished environment should be started.

It is not necessary to cement the filter bottle permanently in place, but filter changing is easier if this is done. Silastic rubber can be used for this purpose. Experiments should first be made to decide upon the best location for the filter and pump. The filter should be placed flat on the tank bottom, with the top of the two vertical slits (shown on page 51) just above the planned water level of the tank. The filter output should be connected to the input fitting of the pump. The pump should be fairly close to the filter, so that it will not be necessary to use too much tubing between the pump and filter.

The thermostatically controlled heater should be mounted on a metal or wood bracket over the tank rim, so that the heating element is as close to the inside tank bottom as possible (without touching it). It should be positioned where there is noticeable water flow. This will ensure its most efficient and effective control of water temperature.

Before putting anything in the tank, the equipment should be checked to be sure that there are no leaks and that the pumping action and water-drop through the vertical slits take place properly. Rocks and filter material can then be put into place.

The next step is to set up a place where the turtles can sun themselves and get warm. In smaller tanks, a rock can be placed on the filter bottle in such a way that the turtles can crawl up onto it to sun themselves. As the rock will be out of the water and the turtles will not be able to reach it, small pieces of flat rock should be cemented together with silastic rubber or epoxy and placed under one edge of the larger rock, like steps, to provide a ramp out of the water, making sure it reaches deep enough into the water. The whole flat rock and ramp assembly must be well balanced on the filter bottle. C-clamps can be used to hold each cemented rock in place until the silastic or epoxy hardens overnight.

In the bigger tanks, a wooden log mounted on tripod legs should be used instead of rock. Logs provide more space and large turtles will not get plastron sores from scraping themselves crawling up the rock.

Bark platform rests on plastic tripod legs. If the bark is very frail, paint a coating of waterproof fiber-glass resin or similar plastic coating on its underside. This also prevents rotting.

Logs take up water room, however, and to prevent this, a ramp can be made of a length of bark that will provide all the sunning space needed for a lot of turtles, as well as a dark place, beneath it, where the turtles can hide. Bark is frail, and must be strengthened with curved, one-inch-wide pine or oak struts to which the bark is silastic-cemented and nailed with finishing nails. The struts are also used to mount the three plastic or wooden-dowel rods that serve as legs and hold the bark ramp in the right position in the tank — two legs at one end, a single leg at the other. Holes should be drilled in the wooden struts at each end of the bark ramp and silastic used to cement the legs into them. Small rubber cups, such as used on tubular metal chair legs, should be put on each leg to prevent the legs from puncturing the tank bottom.

The tank will still look quite bare and so other things should be added to enhance the scene. The filter in big systems should be covered with a large flat rock, if only to hide it from view and to hold it firmly on the bottom. Small-size aquarium gravel should be spread about the bottom in a thin layer not over a half-inch deep. Sand should not be used, as it traps food so that it will not process properly. A few attractive rocks can be added to hide hosing and to add character to the tank bottom. Sharp-edged rocks that might puncture the plastic tank should not be used.

Plants add much to the appearance of the tank, but in big systems with many turtles plants seldom survive. Plastic plants that resemble water varieties are sold in aquarium stores and can be used to create a more natural appearance. Smaller systems will support numerous aquarium-store aquatic plants, as well as such floating garden-pool plants as hyacinth. The light from the sunning lamp will keep them growing. A large lamp is needed for big tanks: A standard 150-watt reflector-bulb spot lamp, in a floor stand, will provide adequate warmth for basking turtles, when the lamp is placed about two and one-half feet away from the bark ramp. It need not be directly overhead, but it might be necessary to use an overhead bracket to hold the lamp in place.

For smaller systems, a gooseneck desk lamp makes an ideal basking lamp. The neck of such a lamp, however, is seldom long enough to reach up and over the tank rim, to the right height, so it should be hung on the wall and the tank should be positioned beneath it. A standard 60-watt bulb, ten to fifteen inches above the rock, will provide the needed warmth for the turtles, and sufficient light to promote plant growth. If the tank is placed near a window, daylight will also help plant growth. There are small-diameter reflector bulbs on the market that can be put in the same lamp to direct more light onto the basking rock. In this case, a 40-watt reflector bulb at the same distance will do just as well as a standard 60-watt bulb.

MAINTENANCE AND FEEDING

A new system should be run for several days before it is stocked with turtles and other life. There might be a number of minor changes and adjustments to make; and an initial check for any possible leakage must be made.

The filter and pump relationship must be worked out. If the water level in the filter goes so far down that the pump sucks air, the water level in the tank may have to be raised to create a greater flow into the filter. If this is not adequate, the gap in one or both vertical slits in the filter bottle should be enlarged, using a very sharp knife or a single-edge razor blade. Care should be used to shave off very little each time, and then the pump action should be tried again.

Should water flow so freely into the filter that there is no drop inside, the water level in the tank should be lowered to restrict the input, or the filter should be put up on a flat rock on the bottom of the tank. If this does not work, it means the slits in the bottle may be too long or too wide. Plastic mylar electrical tape should be fastened around the bottle to close off some of the bottom openings in the slits. When all is working right (with the filtering sponge in place) and the water level in the tank is at a satisfactory level (about one and one-half inches below the rim of the tank), the water level in the filter bottle should be about one-half inch lower than the water level in the tank — and the desired "cascade" of water into the filter will be adequate to cause surface oil to flow into the filter.

When the system is operating well, and the heater is holding the water temperature to about 75° F., or slightly more, put in the tur-

57

The tank water level should be about 1½″ below the tank rim.

tles. They will at first do considerable roaming about and try to climb the sides of the tank. But this is quite normal, for they need time to adjust to their new environment. Leave the sunning lamp on for the night, and when all is quiet, the turtles will in all likelihood emerge from the water. In time, they will settle down and become content with their new home.

The addition of a bottom-feeding turtle — such as a musk or mud turtle — and a Plecostomus catfish will greatly improve the process of keeping things clean. The bottom feeder picks up uneaten scraps of food that fall to the bottom at feeding time, and the catfish spends much of its time cleaning the tank walls, and the backs of the turtles. (This fish is the only one that has enough armor to prevent its being eaten by the turtles.)

Turtles like to snack all the time, but once-a-day feeding is quite all right, and when healthy, a few days off (such as over a weekend when there may be no one home) will not do them any harm.

58

They should be given a wide choice of both animal and plant foods. One of the best choices of steady diet food is Trout Chow, a product of Purina. This is a basic many-ingredient food used by fish hatcheries as an excellent diet for breeding fish that will be used for stocking lakes and rivers. For infant and small turtles, Chow No. 5104, which is a small granular variety of the same food, may be used. For large turtles, the same kind is satisfactory; however, No. 5105 is a larger-pellet food more suited to their mouth size. Both have the advantage of floating on the water until snapped up by the turtles. What is not eaten, or bits dropped by the turtles, sink to the bottom where the bottom feeders pick it up. Food should be given sparingly, so that there is a minimum of waste food for the filter and bacteria to process.

Turtles should be fed small bits of raw fish several times a week. Frozen, unbreaded smelts can be bought in the local supermarket. They are inexpensive, and what is not used may remain frozen indefinitely. While the turtles are being fed the Trout Chow or fish, the filter should be turned off so that none of the floating food flows into it.

Greens should be fed to water turtles, particularly sliders, several times a week (before they are fed fish or Trout Chow on the same day). Of the greens found in supermarkets, they like Boston lettuce, watercress, kale, and lettuce.

While the above foods in combination are a very good diet, bone- and shell-building foods are sometimes not adequately provided. A special gelatin diet that binds together needed supplements, in a form they enjoy, should be fed to the turtles at least once a week. It is a bit tedious to make, but once a batch is made it can be kept in the freezer and used over a six-month period. A recipe for the gel and directions for making it are on page 82.

Cleaning the filter sponges is the main daily chore involved in keeping the tank clean. Where there are only a few turtles in a sys-

Fresh or frozen fish is eaten greedily by water turtles.

A special gelatin should be fed to turtles at least once a week.

tem, this may need to be done only several times a week. The more turtles added, the more often the filter sponges will have to be cleaned. When the sponges have to be cleaned daily, this means that there are about as many turtles as the system can easily support. In a school-room situation, this is probably too many turtles, unless someone can come in to tend them on weekends and holidays.

The filter should be changed when it is so clogged that water no longer cascades into the filter bottle. The sponge will be so clogged with oil and sediment that the pump cannot pull much water through it. The filter sponge should be washed out with soap and water to remove all oil and collected sediment, and rinsed thoroughly. Rotating several filters so each can be allowed to dry out will make them all last longer.

Occasionally, an oil ring will form at the tank waterline — just like a ring in the bathtub. This should be scrubbed away with a toothbrush: the filter will pick up what has been brushed away. Also, aquarium stores sell a small, low-cost battery-operated tank vacuum-cleaner device that will pick up unsightly sediment from the tank bottom.

In time, the rocks in the filter should be removed and cleaned. This is easy and should be done by a quick vigorous rinsing — without soap — in a cool stream of water. This action cleans them without killing the basic culture of bacteria that adheres to the rocks.

Keeping Land Turtles Indoors

To give land turtles all their environmental needs, their container has to be divided into two chambers — one open and one closed. The closed part is tented so as to contain and control the humidity and temperature of its atmosphere. The turtles that live in this setup must, of course, be free to come and go as they wish in the two-part system.

An ideal arrangement of this kind is a penlike open arena that sits upon a table or bureau, or card table. Few land turtles are able to climb over the wall of a container that is higher than their upright reach. And few are inclined to exert enough force to push their way through the walls of their enclosure. For this reason, it is not necessary to cage them in with wire screen or wooden sides. Also, turtles

A healthy land environment for turtles can be built using glass panels, providing an enclosure that is attractively free of opaque walls that obstruct viewing and that would only make it look like an imprisoning chamber.

often injure themselves by scraping their faces against a screen.

The basic platform of the enclosure can be fashioned from plywood. A siding framework is made of aluminum "angle" material. Upon this frame, double-strength window-glass panels can be taped or cemented to provide an upright transparent wall to keep the turtles from wandering off. The picture on page 64 shows the corner detail of such an enclosure. Close-fitting glass panels should be placed around the edges of the arena. Double-side masking tape can be used to secure the glass in the angles, or a clear silastic rubber can be used to cement them in place. Keeping one panel uncemented so it can be slid out aids cleaning. When glass is used, any sharp edges should be sanded down with emery paper. Gloves should be worn when doing this.

Slits in the hanging mylar curtain permit turtles to enter and leave the humidity chamber freely.

The floor of the framework should be constructed like a raised platform. This provides a way to attach the side frames of angle aluminum strips that hold the upright glass. Holes for recessed food and water dishes should be cut in the raised floor. This ensures that the turtles will have good level access to them; also, the dishes can be easily lifted out of their recessed pockets for cleaning. The raised floor also serves to keep the floor temperature higher than usual, and thus guards against chilling.

The most important feature of the turtles' arenalike quarters is a plastic film-enclosed tentlike portion of the arena that is illuminated from above to make it warm and moist. A water dish should be recessed in the tent to provide moisture by evaporation, which makes the inside of the enclosure humid.

The tented enclosure should be covered by a piece of double-strength window-glass from which a length of clear plastic hangs to the floor of the arena, like a curtain. The turtles, of course, have to be able to get in and out of the enclosure, and to make this possible, the plastic curtain will have to be slit at one-inch intervals, from near the top to the bottom. This confines the air inside sufficiently to keep it warm and moist, and allows turtles wishing to enter or leave to walk right through. The strips move aside as the turtles effortlessly pass through the curtain and the strips drop back into place after the turtles have gone through.

The best plastic material to use for the humidity enclosure is clear mylar plastic. It should be thin enough so that the strips cut in it will move fairly easily and not offer too much resistance to the turtles trying to push through them. Saran Wrap will also work, but each hanging strip must be weighted with a small piece of wire solder, because the wrap is so thin and frail that it will not hang straight. However, mylar is best because it springs back into place after a turtle walks through.

Cut the window glass so it neatly covers the humidity enclosure, taping it in place if necessary so that the slit curtain hangs almost to the floor. Since mylar is rigid and springlike, the edge that is taped to the covering glass has to be creased at right angles so that it will hang straight down.

Finish the floor of the arena with waterproof paint or wood sealer. Sand or gravel can be used on the arena floor, but this poses considerable cleaning problems. An ideal flooring cover can be made from thin pebbly plastic matting, which looks like gravel or earth, and can be found in hardware stores. A sheet of this should be trimmed so that it fits easily in place in the arena, and may be easily removed for periodic cleaning.

Cut water and feed dishes from the bottoms of plastic bottles, so

Moisture condensing on the sides of the humidity chamber indicate that there is lots of moisture in the air.

An overhead view of a new arena, with curtain across half of the arena.

that they will fit into the holes cut for them in the raised platform floor (and the matting, if it is also used).

Pieces of bark and rocks in the arena provide a natural setting. A tunnel-like structure of rock and bark is also desirable so that the more timid turtles can hide when they want to. Additional holes should be cut in the floor to accommodate small potted plants, if desired, and provision should be made for sufficient light for the plants.

The most important light over the arena is the one that shines on the humidity enclosure; it evaporates water in the enclosure and keeps it warm. Ordinary low-cost gooseneck desk lamps, with from 25- to 60-watt bulbs, work well for lighting and plant growth. Whatever it will take to hold the humidity chamber to 80°F., or slightly higher, should be used, and a small thermometer should be placed in the tent to check the temperature.

Box turtles are among the many turtles that like to get right into the water, and the water dish in the humidity chamber should be big enough for this. Also, its rim should be flush with the floor, and a small sloping ramp must be provided to make it easy for the turtles to climb out.

In homes where the air is dry, it may be necessary to promote evaporation in the humidity enclosure by using a wick in the water dish. The wick can be made of strips of plastic sponge on a wire. The wick should be in the water dish where it will soak up the water. The light shining on the soaked sponge will increase evaporation of water in the enclosure. A black plastic dish will also promote evaporation, for light shining on it is absorbed and warms the water more effectively than the water in a clear dish.

Two-day-old infant box turtle discovers a worm. In an arena with a humidity chamber, infant box turtles soon settle down to a steady diet of worms, mealworms, hamburger — and sleep.

MAINTENANCE AND FEEDING

Land turtles enjoy both greens and meat foods. Since there is no filtering system to keep their quarters clean, remove uneaten food, lest it spoil. A feeding dish that can be removed easily for frequent cleaning should be used. The arena itself gets dirty fairly often from the waste that the turtles drop and bits of food that get tracked about the enclosure. Replace sand and gravel every several days or rotate this material with some that was removed and washed and thoroughly dried earlier. (Wet sand or gravel must not be used for it will be cold and messy.) Using a plastic mat makes cleanup much easier. It can be lifted out with the dirt that is to be washed away. Two identical

68

mats — for exchange purposes — is a good health investment. One will be allowed to thoroughly dry while the other is being used. The addition of a couple of dry-land hermit crabs from a pet store, which make excellent " housecleaners," will help to keep the area clean and will not harm the turtles.

During cleaning-up, try not to disturb the turtles too much: lift each one aside, slowly, and do the cleaning as quickly as possible. Once a routine has been established, they will get used to it and not be disturbed.

Land turtles like both meats and a wide choice of greens, fresh fruits, and softer vegetables. Hamburger is particularly enjoyed by box turtles, as are earthworms. Young turtles should be offered meat frequently, as they are inclined to require more meat than adults. Mealworms, sold at aquarium and pet stores, are an excellent diet for infant land turtles.

Turtle Health Problems and Special Events

Like all creatures, turtles may get sick. In many cases there may be little that can be done about it. During warm weather, if a turtle's particular problem cannot be taken care of, the kindest thing to do is to release the sick turtle in its home environment — and wish it well. In wintertime, the sick turtle should be treated in isolated quarters, with the hope that any turtle that gets sick will recover. There is always the possibility, however, that some of them may perish.

The best form of turtle health insurance is to make sure that all turtles' routine wants and needs are provided for, in the form of a

The best thing to do for a sick turtle, during warm weather, is to release it in its home environment.

good and plentiful diet and warm clean quarters. They should be kept free of chilling drafts, which can promote respiratory disorders that are often hard to treat and are frequently fatal. And these disorders are usually quite contagious to other turtles.

It is important to avoid exposing a collection of turtles to disease by not introducing a new turtle until its health has been checked. When in doubt, the new turtle should be kept in a separate environment for several weeks to make sure it is free from any contagious disease. A good appetite, proper activity, and normal weight, skin, and eye condition are the main signs of a healthy turtle. Wheezing in its breathing or bubbling moisture coming from its nostrils or mouth suggest that it should not be added to the collection. The

70

chances of its surviving, inside, are poor and the rest of the collection may be infected.

Fungus disorders are a problem when turtles are kept indoors, particularly with water turtles, which are most susceptible when their water is too cool. Keeping their tank water at the right temperature discourages fungus growth. Also, packaged fungicide treatments are sold in aquarium stores. A double-strength dip bath of this can be used to treat badly afflicted turtles. A dip of strong-to-taste salt water, using table salt, is also effective against fungus, plastron sores, and other skin and eye infections. Fifteen-minute treatments, twice a day, are adequate for each infected individual. Be sure that the water used to make either dip — and to rinse them off afterward — is of the same temperature as their tank water.

Eye infection is a common disorder. When turtles have this, their eyes stay closed, and may appear to bulge or be puffed up. There are a number of commercial pet-store preparations, as well as ointments meant to treat human eye-and-ear disorders, that contain antibiotics such as Aureomycin. They come in small metal squeeze tubes, and can be applied, carefully, directly to the affected eye. If the turtle will not open its eyes, the eyelids will have to be gently spread back so that the ointment can be applied to the lids.

There is a liquid eye solution containing Chloromycetin that is easy to apply with a cotton swab or an eyedropper, if a drop can be put right onto the affected eye. Treated water turtles should be kept out of water for several hours after each daily treatment, and all of such infected turtles should be isolated. If the treatment is effective, cure after a week is not unusual.

Getting medicine into a turtle is not easy, for they resist efforts to open their mouths. A plastic eyedropper is the best tool for getting penicillin or tetracycline to the back of the throat of turtles suffering

71

from digestive or respiratory disorders. With small turtles that cannot handle a large dropper, a piece of thin plastic tubing — called spaghetti, and easily obtainable at electronic-supply and model and hobby stores — can be pushed over the end of a glass eyedropper to narrow down the tip so it can be put in the mouth of a small turtle.

Both penicillin and such tetracyclines as Tetrax are often effective in treating unknown digestive and respiratory illnesses. A seemingly healthy turtle that suddenly ceases to eat is usually suffering from such disorders. If it does not resume eating in a week — and it gets listless and slower in its behavior — it should be treated or released.

A commonly found form of penicillin is contained in any of a number of syrup suspensions used to give penicillin to children. With large turtles a quarter of a dropper of this syrup, twice a day, will get useful amounts of penicillin into their system. A single drop is enough for infant turtles. If spillage occurs, wash the turtles off with tepid water — drying land turtles off afterward — before returning them to their quarters.

Tetracyclines are commonly dispensed in 250-milligram capsules that are easily opened to get to the powder inside. As much of this powdered antibiotic as can be stirred into a paste, in a drop of water in a teaspoon, makes an adequate dose for a large turtle (half as much for an infant turtle). Use a wooden match or ice-cream stick to carefully open the turtle's mouth. The antibiotic paste should be gathered on the end of a toothpick and wiped off as far back in the turtle's throat as possible. The turtle's mouth should be held closed for several minutes, so that it does not spit the paste out.

If a sick turtle still eats, putting tetracycline in the gel diet is a good way to get them to take the medicine. Hold aside two ounces of the hot gel mix until it is cool enough to touch. The powder of three 250-milligram capsules should be added to the gel, and, when cool, several small pieces of this can be fed to sick turtles. Like the rest of the gel, it will last a long time in the freezer.

Turtles sometimes get small cuts or other abrasions on their skins or shells. To stop infection, wash the wounds with hydrogen peroxide and cover them with iodine, or an antibiotic ointment. Dab off all excess iodine and be sure it is dry before the water turtles are put back in their tank. Daily treatment keeps sores clean and allows them to heal.

While some of the medicines discussed here are not prescription items, a physician, understanding the difficulty, will usually help by suggesting a needed prescription.

A WORD ABOUT HUMAN HEALTH

Turtles carry few disorders that can seriously affect humans, but there are precautions that should be taken. Turtles can transmit certain intestinal disorders to man. While these disorders are not serious, they can cause diarrhea and stomach cramps. The best insurance against becoming ill from any disorders turtles might convey is to wash your hands in soap and water after handling sick turtles and completing "housekeeping" chores. By always following this simple procedure, one need never contract any disorder turtles have or carry.

SPECIAL EVENTS

One of the rewards for taking the time to set up and maintain a true indoor environment for turtles is natural behavior on their part. For example, it is not unusual for turtles to lay eggs indoors during the winter. If it is suspected that this is likely to happen, it is important to provide an earthen place for them to lay eggs. Without it, they

A cluster of hatchling snappers

will simply drop the eggs in the water and there is the risk of losing them, as other turtles may eat them.

Build a sloping ramp from the tank to a dirt-bottom pen off to one side of the tank, so that a gravid female can leave the water to lay her eggs. The pen should be walled so that the only way out of it is back in the water. Land turtles, for want of dirt in their enclosure, will lay the eggs on the floor of the arena, so recess a large dish of dirt for them in the floor of the pen.

It is best to keep the eggs in a side container where their necessary hatching needs (warmth, clean dampness) are more easily attended to. An ideal "nursery" consists of a flat plastic "cat-litter" tray with about a four-inch rim, filled with rich, slightly moist loam or humus. Keep the tray warm with an overhead lamp. The bulb of a thermometer should be placed in the humus so that the temperature of the nursery can be monitored to about 85–90° F. The external sides of the tray should be insulated with paper or old sheeting, so as to keep the walls of the tray from losing their heat. A piece of glass placed over the top of the tray will keep in heat and moisture.

In nature, the sun warms the earth of a nest of turtle eggs, to as warm as 90° F. At night, it cools down somewhat. Should it rain, the temperature may fall to as low as 70° F. To simulate this, the lamp should be turned off during the day; since indoor temperatures are inclined to be cool at night — particularly in the winter — the heating cycle should be reversed: on at night, off in the day. This will result in a temperature fluctuation in the indoor nest that is not out of line with normal summertime outdoor conditions.

Before burying any eggs in the new nest, the nest should be carefully checked out to make sure it does not get too hot — not more than 90° F. anywhere in the nest (a little above 80° F. is best). If during the test run the nest gets too hot, use a lower-wattage lamp, or move the lamp farther away from the nest.

The eggs should be set close together under half an inch of loose loam. Do not pack the covering in any way. In time, moisture will evaporate, and so the nest must be sprinkled with water every few days to maintain a moist but not wet condition. Up to two months should be allowed for any given batch to hatch. After this, if it appears they are not developing, it may be necessary to sacrifice one egg by opening it to see if it was fertile or not. In any event, if they do not hatch in three months, they may spoil or develop fungus. Throw out any obviously bad eggs that are past due to hatch.

Infant water turtles are best kept alone in their own small system. Many turtles cannot compete with large turtles for food, and so they may starve. Infant land turtles, such as box turtles, need a moist, humid "microclimate" in which to live early in their life. They will thrive in the warm and humid environment of the land-turtle arena's humidity chamber. The feeding of infant land turtles may entail foods that differ from that of the adults, so the infants should be given a wide choice. Box turtle infants, for example, eat almost no vegetable matter for some time, and depend solely upon meat. Earthworms or mealworms are consumed on almost a daily basis, which can be a problem in wintertime, unless there is a small earthworm farm indoors. Infant box turtles, however, can be induced to eat hamburger fairly early in life.

*   *   *   *   *

These may seem to be a rather formidable set of chores to attend to, just to keep a few turtles indoors. But carrying them out becomes quite routine in time. The results are rewarding, for you will have created and will be successfully maintaining — indoors — a miniature portion of their natural outdoor summer environment. The reflection of this achievement is the healthy and natural behavior of the turtles — doing much the same things they would in their own wild, only doing it in someone's home or school — and perhaps when it is snowing outside.

This presents a fine opportunity to study their behavior at its best. If their indoor homes are made as natural-looking as possible, photographs can be taken that will make the turtles look as though they were in their real outdoor environment. And they will be pictures that show them engaged in natural activities that would require great patience and skill to obtain under ordinary field conditions.

Whether kept for study at home or in the schoolroom, or for the simple pleasure of enjoying their company, turtles fare better in an

This natural-looking photograph was taken in a large indoor tank.

indoor or yard environment that is as close as possible to their natural home. The ways and means described here include but a few examples of the kinds of system that can easily be put together with simple materials. With these fundamentals, and a little imagination, it is possible to house a slice of natural environment in which turtles will thrive in an active natural way, and be contented.

Some places where you can find turtles. Above, canvassing an open field for box turtles. Right, searching for painted turtles in a shallow canal bed.

Swampland turtle home. Water turtles are harder to catch than the slow-moving land turtles, as they are quick to hide in the murky depths of the water.

Gel Recipe

Ingredients:

    2 oz. fish (frozen smelt, or any fresh fish)
    8 oz. boiling water
    3 oz. Trout Chow, ground up into a powder
    2 oz. cod-liver oil (found in drug stores)
    1½ oz. unflavored gelatin (found in supermarkets)
    1½ oz. bone meal (found in garden-supply stores)
    1 t. diabasic calcium phosphate (found in drugstores)
    20 drops of red food coloring

Mince the fish into very small pieces. A blender can be used for this. Add the cod-liver oil to the fish and put aside. Dissolve unflavored gelatin into the boiling water, stirring thoroughly. Next, add the minced fish and oil. Then pour in the ground Trout Chow, along with the bone meal and diabasic calcium phosphate. Mix well, adding twenty drops of food coloring. Pour the mix into a shallow pie tin or plastic ice-cube tray and put it in the freezer. Gel should be cut into small cubes or strips to feed to the turtles. Give as much as they will eat at one time. Leftover visible scraps should be netted out of the tank so that they will not have to be processed by the filtration system. Always return uneaten gel to the freezer quickly, covering it with plastic wrap, so that it will not dry out.

Materials List

ITEM	DESCRIPTION	CATALOG OR MODEL	SOURCE
Angle Aluminum	$\frac{1}{2}$" sides angle aluminum recommended for constructing supports for glass-sided land turtle enclosures. Sold in 6' and 8' lengths; available in larger sizes. (Trade-named, Reynolds Aluminum)	#2406	Available in most hardware stores, or call nearest Reynolds Aluminum offices.
Filter Sponges	Polyethylene sponge material sold by the yard as a white foam plastic cushioning or insulation material. Sold as cleaning sponges by supermarkets. Do not use cellulose sponges as they break down in filter.		Hardware or supermarkets
Mylar Film	1 or 2 mm thick mylar is used to make humidity chamber curtain.		DuPont product available in rolls from artist and drafting supply stores. Call local DuPont office for local source.

ITEM	DESCRIPTION	CATALOG OR MODEL	SOURCE
Pumps: #1	200 series centrifugal impeller pump for use in larger tanks. Output approximately 500 gallons per hour (gph). Comes with six-foot line cord, for use on 115 vt 60 Hz.	#2A1-A8BC8F5S8	Gorman-Rupp Ind., Bellville, Ohio 44813
#2	Oscillating pump for use with smaller systems. Delivers approximately 30 gph, from 115 vt 60 Hz.	#Z12500	
#3	Oscillating pump that is very quiet and efficient. Can be used as an inline pump, or can be bulkhead-mounted in the side of container. Three models recommended for different water volume needs. Operates on 115 vt 60 Hz. Trade name is "Fontanette," followed by model #.	CAP 5/1U (for 15 gph) CAP 5/3U (for 25 gph) CAP 5/7U (for 38 gph)	Fountains for the Home, 2921 North 24th Street, Arlington, Va. 22207
#4	Impeller pump made of plastic parts, and which can be submerged in the tank with the turtles. A three-wire cord ensures against shock hazard. Two models; N-100 output is 100 gallon; N-300, 300 gph.	N-100NP (100 gph) N-300NP (300 gph)	Local garden-supply stores, or manufacturer: Thomas Beckett 2521 Willowbrook Rd. Dallas, Texas 75220

ITEM	DESCRIPTION	CATALOG OR MODEL	SOURCE
Trout Meal	Sold in fifty-pound bags. Costs very little per bag and can be divided up with other people who keep turtles. Some aquarium stores will buy it for you and repackage it for general sale.	#5104-a (small pellet) #5105 (larger pellets for bigger turtles)	Agricultural feed stores and some aquarium stores, if requested. Manufacturer: Ralston Purina
Tape: Adhesive both sides	Cloth tape for affixing glass to land-turtle arenas. Available in 1″ rolls.		Polyken products of Kendall Company sold by artist and drafting supply stores.
Silastic	Used for most cementing and sealing chores, such as potting pieces of rock together to form sunning rock on filter, and permanently fixing glass into angle aluminum braces.	Sears' #'s: 9-80832 (clear) 9-80833 (black) 9-80835 (white)	Sears Roebuck & Company
	Also sold by Dow-Corning	RTV-732	Call nearest Dow-Corning office for local source.

BIBLIOGRAPHY

Carr, Archie. *Handbook of Turtles*. Ithaca: Cornell University Press, 1957.

Conant, Roger. *A Field Guide to Reptiles and Amphibians*. Boston: Houghton Mifflin Company, 1958.

Dowling, Herndon G., and Stephen Spencook. *The Care of Pet Turtles*. New York: New York Zoological Society, 1960.

Koschmann, Gale. *Turtle Lore*. Everglades Natural History Association, 1965.

Netting, M. Graham, and Neil D. Richmond, eds. *Pennsylvania Reptiles and Amphibians*. Harrisburg: Conservation Education Division, Commonwealth of Pennsylvania, 1950.

Pope, Clifford. *Turtles of the United States and Canada*. New York: Alfred A. Knopf, 1939.

Pritchard, Peter C. H. *Living Turtles of the World*. Jersey City: T. F. H. Publications, 1967.

Schwartz, Frank J. *Maryland Turtles*. College Park: University of Maryland Natural Resources Institute, 1967.

Stebbins, Robert C. *A Field Guide to Western Reptiles and Amphibians*. Boston: Houghton Mifflin Company, 1966.

Zim, Herbert S., and Hobard M. Smith. *Reptiles and Amphibians*. New York: Golden Press, 1964.

INDEX